ENOUGH OVERTHINKING

DISCOVER 11 INSANE WAYS

11 INSANE WAYS OVERTHINKING CAN AFFECT YOUR HEALTH, DESTROY YOUR HAPPINESS, AND STEAL YOUR JOY – AND HOW TO NEUTRALIZE IT

ROBERT J. CHARLES, PHD, DMIN

ENOUGH OVERTHINKING

11 INSANE WAYS OVERTHINKING CAN AFFECT YOUR HEALTH, DESTROY YOUR HAPPINESS, AND STEAL YOUR JOY AND HOW TO NEUTRALIZE IT

Robert J. Charles

Copyright © 2022 by Robert J Charles

All rights reserved.

It is not legal to reproduce, duplicate, or transmit any part of this document in either electronic means or printed format. Recording of this publication is strictly prohibited and any storage of this document is not allowed unless with written permission from the publisher except for the use of brief quotations in a book review.

The content contained within this book may not be reproduced, duplicated or transmitted without direct written permission from the author or the publisher.

Under no circumstances will any blame or legal responsibility be held against the publisher, or author, for any damages, reparation, or monetary loss due to the information contained within this book. Either directly or indirectly. You are responsible for your own choices, actions, and results.

Legal Notice:

This book is copyright protected. This book is only for personal use. You cannot amend, distribute, sell, use, quote, or paraphrase any part, or the content within this book, without the consent of the author or publisher.

Disclaimer Notice:

Please note the information contained within this document is for educational and entertainment purposes only. All effort has been executed to present accurate, up-to-date, reliable, and complete information. No warranties of any kind are declared or implied. Readers acknowledge that the author is not rendering legal, financial, medical, or professional advice. The content within this book has been derived from various sources. Please consult a licensed professional before attempting any techniques outlined in this book.

By reading this document, the reader agrees that under no circumstances is the author responsible for any losses, direct or indirect, which are incurred as a result of the use of the information contained within this document, including, but not limited to, — errors, omissions, or inaccuracies.

Contents

Introduction 3
Overthinking 6
What Is Overthinking, Anyway? 8
Anxiety, Worry, and Self-Doubt 10
Stress 12
Three Forms of Overthinking 15
Summary 19
Key Takeaways 21
Time to Take Action 23
Part I: Physical Effects 25
    Impact on the Digestive System 27
    Impact on the Skin 29
    Impact on the Immune System 30
    Key Takeaways 30
    Time to Take Action 32
Part II: Mental Effects 34
    Impact on the Brain 36
    Impact on Daily Life 39
    Impact on Sleep 41
    Impact on Work 42
    Impact on Energy Levels 44
    Key Takeaways 46

Time to Take Action 47
Part III: Social Effects 51
    Impact on Time 53
    Impact on Joy 55
    Impact on Self-Esteem 55
    Key Takeaways 56
    Time to Take Action 57
Part IV: Moving Forward 60
    Effective Strategies to Stop Overthinking 64
    How to Develop and Maintain a Healthy Mindset 76
    Key Takeaways 81
    Time to Take Action 82
Conclusion 84
Thank You 86
References 87

DO YOU WANT TO DISCOVER HOW TO DEAL WITH DIFFICULT PEOPLE?

These **3 FREE** offers are exactly for you: 2 audiobooks + 1 e-book.

You will also get the 'Enough Overthinking' audiobook.

<<Just click right here to discover Powerful Technics to Keep Toxic People in check>>

Inside these 2 audiobooks and 1 e-book, YOU will discover:

- The types of toxic people and how to escape their web of crises.
- More about Highly Sensitive Persons and their relationships with High Conflict Persons.
- The three different forms of overthinking and how to spot them.
- How ruminating and worries can damage your social life.

If you want to know how to deal with difficult people,

Click here to get these 3 FREE offers.

OTHER BONUS

How to Face any Challenge with Confidence?

Download these **FREE 30 BIBLICAL PROMISES** to discover some powerful promises for **YOU**.

Click: https://go.robertjcharles.com/30BiblicalPromises

At some point, everyone on this Earth faces a tough challenge. Help is on the way! God has your back. His Word will empower you to face any trial or tribulation. These 30 promises from God will give you the strength and resilience you need to move forward.

To get your **FREE** 30 BIBLICAL PROMISES TO OVERCOME ANY CHALLENGE, **click on this link:**
https://go.robertjcharles.com/30BiblicalPromises

Introduction

"Do not be anxious about anything, but in every situation, by prayer and petition, with thanksgiving, present your requests to God. And the peace of God, which transcends all understanding, will guard your hearts and your minds in Christ Jesus."

— Philippians 4:6-7 (NKJV)

It's 6 p.m. and you've just finished a long day at work. As you drive home, you're still processing the day, but you're also thinking about the important project with the looming deadline at the end of the month. Your manager has been putting pressure on you to get it done, and you're already stressed about it. What if you can't finish it in time? What if you end up losing your job over it? Then you start thinking about what a terrible impact losing your job would have on your financial situation, and your thoughts continue to spiral out of control until you've worked yourself into a state of high anxiety.

Does this scenario sound familiar? Do all of the things you need to do and remember overwhelm you? Do you constantly worry you're missing something important or struggling to keep up with everything going on in your life? Do you obsess over problems and immediately jump to the worst-case scenario? If you have trouble tuning out your racing thoughts, leading you to feel tired and troubled on a regular basis, you're probably a chronic overthinker. You may start to feel trapped in a mental prison, overthinking problems that could easily be solved if only you could break out of your anxiety. As an old African proverb says, "When there is no enemy within, the enemy outside can do you no harm."

Overthinking has become an international epidemic in recent years, as we live in increasingly challenging and demanding times that require a great deal of mental capacity just to function as adults. Daily responsibilities, work, worries about money, emotional trauma, and other issues keep our minds engaged 24 hours a day. Due to the fast-paced, demanding nature of modern life, everyone overthinks from time to time, and that's normal—whether it's about family, health, children, your mortgage, a better future, or career expectations. That said, if you get caught in this spiral, you might start to feel doing nothing is preferable to taking a chance and facing the unknown consequences of your decisions. Overthinking becomes an issue at this point.

The most powerful force you will ever encounter is your mind. If you let it, your mind is capable of deceiving you, persuading you that you're unable to do something, that you're not cut out for it, you're not qualified, you just can't do it. This book will help you to recognize the harmful effects of overthinking—physically, mentally, and socially—and to confront the mental processes that are leading you to overthink, allowing you to calm your mind and discover peace. Remember, God does not want you to overthink. He is in control of your life.

> *"The Lord said to me:*
> *You can set down your burden.*
> *He will sustain you; you will never falter."*
>
> **– Psalm 55:22 (NKJV)**

There is a certain power in the human mind, but when it's focused on negative thinking or destructive behavior, that power becomes a weapon. We are all capable of free will, free thought, and imagination, but if we don't use them righteously and positively, the mind can turn them against us. Many of the stresses we face in life are brought upon us by our own imagination, when we imagine an anxiety-inducing scenario over and over until it takes on a life of its own. If you fear something because you've imagined it so intensely, it will eventually ruin your peace.

Overthinking

"Trust in the Lord with all your heart; do not depend on your understanding. Seek his will in all you do, and he will show you which path to take."

– Proverbs 3:5-6 (NKJV)

Overthinking. It's the sleepless nights caused by past regrets that continue to haunt you. It's worrying about the future as you brood over negative experiences in the past. It's every paralyzing fear. It's constantly worrying that you'll fail a class, a job, a relationship, or life. It's endlessly asking yourself what you've done wrong and how you can fix it.

Overthinking is the pause between texts as you wonder how the other person interpreted what you wrote. It's typing out an entire text and then deleting it because you're not comfortable with what you've written. It's the never-ending need for answers and responses to keep your mind satisfied. It's caring too much about other people's opinions. It's getting upset with yourself for questioning and thinking the worst of people.

Overthinking is the critical voice that brings you down because it doubts everybody and everything around you, especially yourself. It's being unable to trust your gut feeling.

It's believing the scary scenarios your mind creates, even when other people tell you they're totally unrealistic. It's helplessly following your own mind down a self-destructive road. It's like an uncontrolled wildfire, destroying everything in its path.

As you can see, overthinking is much more than simply thinking too much about something. It can quickly take over your life if you let it.

Unfortunately, many people are stuck in this way of thinking, not because they lack self-control or willpower—but because we live in a society that encourages us to overthink everything. Additionally, we tend to focus on the bad more than the good because our brains are programmed to pay more attention to negative things as a safety mechanism. However, when we overthink our past mistakes and failures, or worry about future ones, it can lead us down a path of anxiety and depression.

What Is Overthinking, Anyway?

We've described many symptoms of overthinking above, but it can officially be defined as thinking excessively and for long periods of time about an anxiety-inducing event. It is different from problem-solving because problem-solving involves thinking about a solution, whereas overthinking involves dwelling far too much on the problem itself.

Overthinking is an automatic habit over which we have little conscious control. Our brains are wired for overthinking since all our memories, thoughts, and emotions are interconnected in spiderweb-like networks. Although the ability to connect a variety of thoughts and emotions makes us more effective thinkers and allows us to avoid painful outcomes (criticism, rejection, failure, illness, etc.) through learning from our previous experiences, it can also paralyze our decision-making.

You can check whether you've crossed the overthinking threshold using the following criteria: perfectionism, insomnia, fatigue, demanding feedback on insignificant topics, irritability, hypochondriasis, and/or persistent sadness and negative thinking. If you take time to reflect on which of these symptoms are showing up for you, you've taken the first step toward correcting your overthinking problem by recognizing that there is, in fact, a problem.

Let's now look at three of the main symptoms of overthinking: anxiety, worry, and self-doubt.

Anxiety, Worry, and Self-Doubt

Anxiety is a very familiar emotion for overthinkers. Anxiety is defined as an unpleasant, restless feeling, usually expressed through nervous behavior such as physical discomfort, pacing, or tics. It involves fear and apprehension of about the future, sometimes leading to panic or feelings of impending doom. Anxiety and overthinking usually go hand in hand, and in some cases, overthinking may lead to or be the result of an anxiety disorder.

One of the most common symptoms of an anxiety disorder is the tendency to overthink. The brain is constantly on edge, hyperaware, on guard for anything it deems unsafe or troubling. Overthinkers see issues even when there aren't any, and it's anxiety that causes them to feel that way.

Worry is strongly connected to anxiety and refers broadly to having continual, frantic images or feelings about a specific negative outcome in your mind. For example, you may continually and frantically imagine failing your exam tomorrow, and because of this worry, you start thinking about how you can avoid that scenario. However, often the looming worry of actually failing your exam results in feelings of distress and dread that grip you and won't let go.

Self-doubt, on the other hand, is slightly different; it is a pervasive lack of confidence and a sense that you will fail at a new pursuit you wish to undertake because you feel you aren't experienced or skilled enough to accomplish your goal.

Stress

As you can see, these co-morbid symptoms of overthinking (anxiety, worry, and self-doubt) can have huge impacts on the body and the mind, and all three are linked to the body's reaction to stress.

Stress is a physical, mental, or emotional agent that responds to bodily or mental strain. It is the body's way of protecting itself from any imminent threat by switching into an automatic response best known as the "fight-or-flight" response.

The fight-or-flight response is intended to help you stay focused, energized, and aware in a potentially life-threatening situation to have the best chance of survival. It sends adrenaline, cortisol, and other hormones surging through your body to provide you with additional strength to defend yourself from an attack, or to give you the wherewithal to quickly slam on your brakes to avoid a car accident.

Stress also gives you the capability to tackle obstacles. It's what keeps you motivated during exam time when you'd rather be slacking off. The stress hormones that get released sharpen your concentration and drive you to accomplish everything on your schedule.

In cases like these, stress is a normal and even beneficial part of life that everyone experiences. Stress often helps us to push through a difficult day.

But, at some point, you can be under too much stress, and that's when it's no longer beneficial. At this moment, the pressure begins to cause major damage to your physical and mental health and wellbeing. And these days, with our hectic, competitive, internet-fueled lives, there are more opportunities for overwhelming stress to occur than ever before—from career expectations and financial strain to relationships and social media.

In fact, many of us are probably in a constant state of stress. It might feel like you just can't unwind at the end of the day because these stressors are ever-present, leaving you to automatically overthink things in an attempt to find a solution amidst this ocean of anxiety and self-doubt. With so many demands affecting every aspect of your life, it's no wonder you may be spending sleepless nights ruminating over your problems and feeing paralyzed by anxiety. This is especially true when it comes to taking decisive action, as thinking about the numerous potential negative outcomes immobilizes your decision-making ability.

This mental habit paralyzes you from taking action in your life. It also drains your energy and throws you into a never-ending loop of thinking the same thoughts again and again. This cyclical thinking uses up all your time and energy and prevents you from making decisions, trying new things, and progressing in life. It's like a hamster running on its wheel, going round and round but remaining in the same place.

Social media and the internet only exacerbate this "analysis paralysis" by providing an unrealistic and idealized version of life. The result is a "perfect" standard that we feel obligated to meet in order to fit in, but of which we always fall short no matter what, resulting once again in endless anxiety, worry, and self-doubt. (If you want to see examples of this unrealistic standard, look no further than your Instagram feed.)

Of course, we all hope to be successful in many important aspects of our lives, but more often than not, we don't have that kind of power. We can't control our partners, bosses, children, markets, or the economy, all of which can impact our lives. What we *can* control, however, is our own thinking and how we react to all of these stressors.

At this point, it's important to note that overthinking can often be a symptom of an underlying mental health condition such as depression, trauma, PTSD, agoraphobia, or an anxiety disorder characterized by constant and excessive stress, worrying, and dwelling on the past. If you think this might be the case, it's important that you seek help from a mental health professional.

Three Forms of Overthinking

Now that you know the symptoms and effects of overthinking, let's examine three dangerous forms of overthinking—ruminating, fear, and excessive worrying.

Ruminating—Rehashing the Past

Ruminating is obsessively going over a thought or problem repeatedly without ever coming to a conclusion. Whether it be repeating an old argument in your mind over and over or mentally replaying a mistake you made like a broken record, you just cannot seem to let the thought go no matter what. Ruminating is heavily connected with depression because this mental health condition causes you to remember the worst aspects of yourself continually.

You can see the self-defeating aspect of ruminating. It's one of the most dangerous things about overthinking because it paralyzes you and prevents you from taking action. What's the point if (according to your mind) you're just going to fail, no matter how hard you try, or it's already too late to turn things around from a previous bad decision? As you can see, rumination reflects how you views yourself and is thus deeply rooted in self-esteem and self-image.

If you've experienced any form of abuse, neglect, or trauma, it could result in lower self-esteem or self-image. This is further exacerbated if you have a history of academic, athletic, or social underperformance during your formative years and have been constantly compared to your higher-performing peers. Without any obvious talents to make you think otherwise, it's easy to feel like you're a nobody.

Fear for the Present

Fear for the present actually stems from the past. It is a reminder that things can be taken away in an instant and there is nothing you can do about it. If you find yourself constantly in a state of fear about what could happen to you or a loved one at any moment, you are experiencing this form of overthinking.

This feeling activates when you have something important on your mind and don't want anything else to stand in its way, whether it's a relationship or a work project. The fear hinders your productivity because you're constantly worrying about danger or failure. The anxiousness associated with this fear makes it difficult to concentrate on key tasks.

Another reason we may find it difficult to live in the present is that it is constantly filled with reminders of our mortality. Whether we realize it or not, we become acutely aware of life's relentless course. Change is the only constant.

However, if you relive the same scenario over and over again, whether it's about to happen or has already happened, you are being consumed by your thoughts. If you tend to get caught up in negative visions of the future, you are locked in "worry mode." We all do this to some degree, but the critical question is whether or not you have moved into addictive thinking territory. Just like an addiction to substances consumes a person with anxiety, worry, and doubt, being addicted to overthinking and overanalyzing creates a sense of being bound to suffering. It takes you over, and it isn't very easy to be present and in your body.

Why does this happen? Because underneath the fear, subtle or not, emotions are begging to be processed. For example, if you are nervous about an upcoming conversation, rather than being with and facing the fear, your brain will run every possible scenario to try to make you feel that you can control the outcome—to try to make you feel secure. This is not realistic. Don't be trapped by this false promise. The reality is, we can't control what happens in life and it's better to learn to live without the fear.

Excessive Worrying—Predicting the Future Negatively

Worry is your brain anticipating potential problems in order to avoid them, but this tends to lead to negative, usually disastrous future predictions:

- I'm going to fail the test tomorrow. I'll blank out, forget everything, and end up failing out of school.

- I'll never get my dream job. There's always going to be someone better than me. I should play it safe and work a stable and well-paying career I hate.

As you can see, ruminating and worrying are closely related; both cause one to think negatively, whether it be about oneself or a situation.

You may feel stressed about your presentation tomorrow, so you start to tell yourself that you won't do a good job. The more you think about it, the more you worry about what could go wrong, and the worse you feel. Or perhaps you have low self-esteem and feel that you aren't good enough, so you constantly worry that your spouse or partner will find someone else and leave you. Because you don't believe in yourself, you don't have confidence in how things will turn out; you are therefore always worrying about the future—fear of the unknown.

Summary

Overthinkers imagine the worst-case scenarios and get anxious based on these "visions." It's one thing to occasionally have some negative thoughts or to sometimes worry about the future or ruminate on the past, but it becomes a problem when these thoughts or even images start playing repeatedly in your mind.

For example, imagine you're going to grab your kids from school; you have five minutes before they'll be outside waiting for you. On the way to their school, your car breaks down, and now you have to call for help. Your mind shows you an image or "vision" that your kids are waiting, no one is there to pick them up, and then some stranger comes along, entices the kids into his car, and now your kids are gone.

You then start feeling anxious, and your mind starts accusing you of being a bad parent or caregiver. This is the trap of overthinking. When this happens, stop and take a moment to identify the trick your mind is playing on you, then determine how you can solve the problem. In our example of picking up the kids, you could call AAA, then call the school and let the principal know what happened, and finally make a call to a trusted friend or family member who can go to pick up your children.

When you take a moment to reflect and think about the best-case scenario, your mind doesn't have time to stress over irrational scenarios that are most likely not going to happen.

Studies suggest that overthinking leads to mental health issues and poor sleep, which in turn can lead to alcohol or drug use as a way to cope. So, let's dive into figuring out how to put an end to this ruminating, over-worrying nightmare. Practice these strategies for some peace and quiet up there, and more restful nights:

Key Takeaways

- Overthinking is the habit of continually analyzing and reflecting on an experience or a situation to the detriment of one's mental or physical health.

- Overthinking usually occurs in three forms: rumination, fear, and excessive worry, which are self-defeating patterns in our lives.

- Rumination is a pattern of cyclical thinking that happens automatically and constantly. It is characterized by repeating the same thought without ever coming to a conclusion, usually accompanied by negative feelings and anxiety.

- Fear is a reaction to a present, perceived threat, and it impacts one both physically and emotionally. We find it difficult to live in the present if it is constantly filled with reminders of our mortality.

- The worries that our forefathers instilled in us, as well as worries about current events, create a stress response in the brain.

- We live in uncertain times! If you're determined to try to make your life completely certain and predictable, you'll be trapped in fear and you won't be able to live in the moment and enjoy the good things that come your way.

- Worrying itself is an attempt to anticipate a negative outcome that may never occur. Once you've accepted the idea of something bad happening, it will constantly be in your mind. This phenomenon may be linked to an anxiety disorder and can be treated with therapy.

- Overthinking causes us to dwell on the negative part of an event or experience, making us so fearful of the unknowable future that we would rather live in our present moment. By contrast, problem-solving allows us to dwell on the positive part of an event or experience.

- You should stop ruminating over negative thoughts, no matter how hard it is to let them go, because ruminating has such detrimental effects on your life.

- Everyone spends some time overthinking. Our brain is programmed to think in steps. But you should try your best not to stay in this overthinking mode for too long.

Time to Take Action

Think about your life and how much time you spend overthinking. Do you find yourself spending far too much time ruminating over things that have happened in the past, or perhaps worrying about the future so much that it prevents you from enjoying the present?

Try to think back to a time when you had a difficult experience and consider how you reacted to it. Did you spend any amount of time contemplating it (or worrying about it) beforehand? Did worrying stop the negative thing from happening or help you recover faster?

Naturally, we have to think before making any decision, but we do not have to overthink it. God wants us to pray about stressful situations rather than to overthink them. He is your Father. He will take care of you.

In the Bible, we can see King David facing tough situations. He wrote:

> *"Cast your burden on the Lord,*
> *And He shall sustain you;*
> *He shall never permit the righteous to be moved."*
>
> **– Psalm 55:22 (NKJV)**

In this Psalm, David starts by pouring out his soul before his God. In verse 2, he begs, *"Attend to me, and hear me; I am restless in my complaint, and moan noisily."* Verse 17 shows us how David handles his challenges by reaching out to God:

> *"Evening and morning and at noon*
> *I will pray, and cry aloud,*
> *And He shall hear my voice."*
>
> **– Psalm 55:17 (NKJV)**

As David did, you can go boldly to God in prayer. He is always available to listen as if you were the only one on Earth talking to Him. Put your burdens in His Mighty Hands. He is our loving God. He loves you. He will take good care of you.

In the following chapters, we will consider the physical, mental, and social effects of overthinking and examine overthinking in light of what the Bible says.

PART I

Physical Effects

"Therefore, do not worry about tomorrow, for tomorrow will worry about its own things. Sufficient for the day is its own trouble."

– Matthew 6:34 (NKJV)

When you let your mind explore the countless possibilities of a future riddled with worries and concerns, is it possible that you are detrimentally impacting your health?

In short: Yes. Countless studies have been done showing that stress and rumination (i.e., overthinking) take a huge toll on our mental and physical health if we let them.

The reality is, stress is a constant. Stressors will always be a part of our lives. It's going to be difficult to pay the bills. There will always be a few people in our lives with whom we're more likely to argue, people who irritate us or with whom we just can't get along. And of course, accidents are always possible—a flood in the basement, a damaged AC unit, a fender bender. These are all very common stressors and are quite real. We can't control these events, but we can control our stress. We will live in misery if we don't.

Many people have trouble managing stress. They believe that a happy life means living without any stress or anxiety. That is not true. There are strategies you can use to manage and live with the inevitable stress that comes and goes throughout life. You can even use stress to find a better solution or a healthier way of living. You can learn more about yourself by using stress to better solve your problems. There is no waiting for a better future; it's time to use what you already have and make the most of it.

To do so, you need to be able to distinguish between stress and stressor. Stress is your emotional response to a stressor. Your response is what causes stress. While outside influences may be powerful, you can remain in control of your emotional reaction.

When we're able to view stressors in a positive light, it's called stress management. If you're stressed at work, rather than thinking, "I can't do this!", look at the situation and ask yourself, "What can I do to make this better?" This type of "good" stress acts as a motivator.

Consider the difference between going on vacation and going to work every morning. Both of these activities can be stressful. It's just as stressful to pack, plan flights, find hotels, and prepare for a trip as it is to handle your daily tasks and problems at work. The difference is your perspective. We perceive vacation as an enjoyable event, and therefore we're able to handle the stressors of planning and packing much better than we typically handle work stressors.

Your perception of the stressors you face will determine how well you can overcome them. Managing your emotional response to the circumstances in which you find yourself will enable you to live a happier, more peaceful life.

This chapter will examine the physical effects of overthinking by exploring the correlation between its negative emotional side effects and its physical impact on one's health.

Impact on the Digestive System

It had been five days since Amy last saw Tyler, and still, the worry wouldn't leave her. Day and night, she thought about their last encounter, about the words they'd exchanged and the lie that had slipped out before she could even think about what she was saying. She knew the fact that it wasn't premeditated was no excuse, though; she had lied to Tyler, and she hadn't amended it. And now that she would soon be seeing him again, the lie was twisting a knot in her stomach.

When Amy woke up after another restless night of thinking about the lie over and over, she made her breakfast like she did every day. Her stomach already felt uneasy. What if she told Tyler the truth and he didn't forgive her? What if, when the time came, she didn't have the courage to tell him the truth? What if he thought she was a pathological liar and cast her out of his life? What if she couldn't make things right? What if…? The "what ifs" kept dancing in her mind, as restless as she was. The same breakfast she ate every morning made its way down Amy's throat, and with it came a familiar sensation—burning.

Not thinking about it too much, Amy grabbed an antacid and took it with a glass of water, unaware that the reason for her heartburn was the racing of her mind. After endlessly thinking about her mistake, day and night, for almost a whole week, the stress of overthinking was taking a toll on her digestive system.

If Amy had talked with Tyler straightaway instead of mulling over her lie for days, she could have avoided this pain and discomfort altogether. She was afraid to tell Tyler the truth because she didn't want to be perceived as a liar, but her fear made her delay telling him and only caused her to feel guiltier and more nervous, which caused her stomach pain.

So, what's the moral of the story here?

As ruminate and worry over a problem, stress starts taking over. You won't be able to relax or stop the thoughts racing through your head long enough to enjoy a meal. Your digestive process takes a backseat because your brain is completely focused on what you're stressing about. A little bit of stress won't cause any real damage to the digestive system; you may just experience some short-term discomfort. However, when you allow stress to fester over long periods of time, you'll start to experience long-term side effects, such as heartburn, indigestion, and constipation, that can eventually wreak havoc on your body.

Stress is also a common reason that people can't maintain a healthy weight. Because of the stress hormones coursing through your body, your digestive system does not function efficiently and takes longer to absorb food. While you're eating dinner, the body is still trying to digest your lunch. And while dinner is being digested, it's already time for bed. (This goes back to the fight-or-flight response we discussed in the previous chapter; if your body thinks it needs to prepare you to either fight or flee a situation because of high stress levels, its priority is no longer making sure your food is well-digested.)

Impact on the Skin

When your body is under constant stress and worry, it can cause the skin to become irritated. This irritation, in turn, could produce other skin conditions such as eczema or psoriasis, which are common health problems among those who have been diagnosed with anxiety or depression. Eczema and psoriasis are difficult and painful conditions to manage and can take years to go away, even with proper treatment.

Impact on the Immune System

Overthinking is the number one trigger of immune system dysfunction. When you're always thinking about things that make you feel fearful, your body goes into attack mode (fight-or-flight), leaving you more vulnerable to viruses and bacteria because, once again, your body is not focused on fighting germs if it thinks your life is in danger.

Today's modern lifestyle puts tremendous strain on the immune system, and as a result, it can become weakened over time, causing sickness after sickness. The stress created by illness can also cause the immune system to develop pro-inflammatory substances that act as a warning to the body's defense mechanisms of future dangers, thus leading to chronic inflammation and illness.

When your immune system becomes weakened due to stress, it is less effective at fighting off an infection, and you are more likely to get sick. If you don't sleep well, suffer from chronic pain, or have constant aches and pains throughout the day (all of which can be side effects of stress and overthinking), you are also more likely to get sick.

Key Takeaways

- Overthinking can lead to stress, which can hurt your digestive system. Inflammatory bowel illnesses, irritable bowel syndrome, abnormalities in gastric acid secretion, poor nutrient absorption, and abnormalities in the intestinal microbiota are all symptoms of stress.

- Overthinking and worrying can jeopardize your cardiovascular health, resulting in chest pain, tachycardia (rapid heartbeat), lightheadedness, and other issues. Depression, generalized anxiety disorder, misuse of alcohol or drugs, and sleep problems, all of which are linked to chronic worrying, can exacerbate the condition.

- The skin is affected by constant anxiety, stress, and overthinking. Worrying causes emotional stress, aggravating various skin conditions like psoriasis, atopic dermatitis (eczema), alopecia (hair loss), and seborrheic dermatitis. Stress produces inflammation in the body, which results in skin flare-ups. Chronic stress affects the complex, interrelated endocrine and immune systems, exacerbating skin problems.

- Have you ever noticed how easily you become sick when you're upset or anxious? Stress leads the body to release cortisol, which weakens the immune system. When your body's natural defenses are weakened, you're more susceptible to infection and disease.

Time to Take Action

Are you always trying to read between the lines, finding more things to worry about in what should be a straightforward situation? Do you suffer from insomnia? Do you notice more aches and pains during times of stress and anxiety? Have you been accused of being an overthinker at least once? If any of these questions describe you, you might be an overthinker. Worriers just can't stop themselves from overanalyzing everything, but it has truly detrimental effects both mentally and physically.

Keep in mind that continual overthinking and anxiety may be claiming more than your mental tranquility. When your mind is always in flux, your body produces more cortisol, resulting in long-term consequences for your health. This is what happens when you overthink everything.

Life is full of surprises. Sometimes the unexpected happens. But do not worry; God is in control of your life. In Psalm 31, David describes how a situation has affected his being:

> *"Have mercy on me, O Lord, for I am in trouble;*
> *My eye wastes away with grief,*
> *Yes, my soul and my body!*
> *I am forgotten like a dead man, out of mind;*
> *I am like a broken vessel."*

– Psalm 31:9, 12 (NKJV)

But even in his despair, David did not continue overthinking the problem. He did only one thing: he went to God in prayer. With faith, he believed that he would be delivered from this problem. He writes:

> *"But as for me, I trust in You, O Lord;*
> *I say, 'You are my God.'*
> *My times are in Your hand;*
> *Deliver me from the hand of my enemies,*
> *And from those who persecute me.*
> *Make Your face shine upon Your servant;*
> *Save me for Your mercies' sake."*
>
> **– Psalm 31:14-16 (NKJV)**

The only thing you have to do is to ask and reclaim His promise with faith in the name of Jesus. It's time to come out of this sea of overthinking, where you are continually floundering. Start living a life of joy.

Now that we've seen some of the physical effects of overthinking, let's dig into the mental effects.

PART II

Mental Effects

"Have mercy on me, O Lord, for I am in trouble;
My eye wastes away with grief,
Yes, my soul and my body!
I am forgotten like a dead man, out of mind;
I am like a broken vessel."

– Psalm 31:9, 12 (NKJV)

Do you ever find yourself lying awake for hours, unable to stop thinking about something that happened earlier in the day? Do you second-guess practically all of the decisions you've made in your life? Is your career or your social life becoming too much for you because of how much time you spend overanalyzing every aspect of it?

After reading this chapter, you will be aware of where your mental chatter comes from and how you can calm your noisy mind.

Although stress can affect our brains in many ways, let's first look at how it happens. We actually learn how to stress out as children, just as we learn and imitate other types of responses we see from authority figures in our life, like empathy, concern, anger, or joy. Imagine a child trips and falls down. If a caregiver responds with concern and fear, the child may cry. If, however, the caregiver smiles, helps the child up, and gently says, "You're okay," the child is more likely to realize that he or she is actually okay and recover faster.

Our brain is often seen as a single organ similar to the stomach or heart, each of which has a single function. This is not true of the brain, however. Your brain is composed of many parts that work together to form one harmonious organ. The left side of the brain, for example, is responsible for logic and reasoning, while the right side is responsible for creativity. The hippocampus in particular is a crucial area of the brain that is affected by stress. This area is responsible for memory storage, learning new things, and regulating emotions. The neurons that form our memories in the hippocampus can be destroyed by chronic stress—in fact, stress can even cause your hippocampus to shrink, which increases anxiety over time (Cherry, 2021).

Your brain is the control center, the root of everything that happens in your body. It can work with the rest of your organs to improve your overall health—but if you allow yourself to become overwhelmed by stress, it can cause your brain to stop functioning properly in terms of applying rational thought to difficult situations.

After all, it's hard to make decisions when you're in a state of panic. Imagine you have an upcoming work deadline that has been taking over your thoughts for weeks. The closer the deadline gets, the more panicked you feel, until you can't even use basic problem-solving strategies to help you meet the deadline because your mind goes completely blank with fear whenever you think about it (and you think about it all the time).

As you can see, your brain will change and can even be damaged if you remain in a state of stress for too long. Now, don't start panicking that you're killing neurons because you're stressed; no one can ever be completely stress-free, and it's fine to feel a little anxious or worried from time to time. However, it's essential to remember that you only have one brain in this life, so you need to treat it with respect. The good news is your anxious, overthinking mind can be retrained and rewired to be less anxious and more at peace.

Impact on the Brain

The brain contains approximately 100 billion neurons, and each neuron has an average of 7,000 synapses (connections to other neurons). All our thoughts and experiences are stored in the brain as memories, and every time we recall a specific memory, those synapses are strengthened. The more often we access these memories, the quicker and easier it is to bring up those thoughts and feelings (Wolff, 2019). This means that if you store a lot of negative thoughts and memories, and continually bring them to mind, it will only get easier to think negatively each time you do so. With this idea in mind, how else does overthinking affect the brain?

In recent years, researchers at Stanford University have been investigating the link between the brain and increased creativity. Studies have found that when we overthink, it can actually decrease our creativity (Bergland, 2022). The implication here is that overthinking a problem can actually be counterproductive, as it prevents us from coming up with creative new solutions.

It's not just creative thinking that's affected, though. When we encounter stress coming from many different angles—such as from work, family dynamics, and friendships—we have a harder time dealing with it. The combination of stressors creates more "mental clutter," which makes it easy to feel overwhelmed, especially if we lack the right coping methods that might otherwise help us sort through and deal with all of the sources of stress.

Overthinking is a form of mental clutter that clouds our ability to see things clearly. Perhaps you're familiar with how taxing it is to overthink literally everything, from what to eat for dinner to the conversation you had with a coworker yesterday to how to approach your next relationship. This constant anxiety drains the brain and leads to stress and depression. It renders our brain cells incapable of discovering innovative solutions.

It is natural to have negative thoughts at times; your brain automatically generates them as a survival mechanism. These automatic negative thoughts can be overwhelming and may make you feel anxious and depressed. However, you can deal with them and change the narrative. You have the power to change the way your mind works and to reset your default way of thinking to positive.

How?

Well, consider that although our brain is an organ, it acts as a muscle in the sense that it can be trained and strengthened. If you're an overthinker, it simply means that your brain has been trained in the wrong way, through no fault of your own. As an example, we know from biological research that negative thoughts are processed in the right prefrontal cortex, above the right eye. Thanks to brain-scanning technology, scientists have discovered that people who suffer from depression have an overdeveloped right prefrontal cortex. It's essentially the same thing as lifting weights with only your right arm—it will become overpowered, and your left will never be able to keep up. So, how can you blame your brain for having negative thoughts when that's what it's been trained to do?

To reverse the bad habit, you'll need to put effort into retraining your brain to store and access more positive memories and thoughts. Fostering empathy for humanity, a desire to help others every day, and greater awareness of the needs of others is a great way to start living a life full of meaning and joy rather than fear. Unfortunately, many fall into the trap of overthinking, which leads to anxiety—a feeling that threatens happiness and halts the flow of positivity in our lives.

Impact on Daily Life

Worry brings self-doubt and constant fear of the unknown, making it difficult to accept and embrace changes in our lives. Fear causes us to avoid things we want to do by trapping us in our minds in an attempt to keep us safe.

However, in circumstances that are not actually dangerous, fear is often an illusion created by the mind. When we fear change or the unknown or the judgment of others, we miss the opportunities that are right in front of us—be it a promotion, meeting someone new, or the chance to gain knowledge that will make us better in some way.

We'll talk more about fear and how to control it later. For now, let's focus on the fact that despite the fact that most of us logically recognize that our fear is irrational, we are not at ease. Even the modern luxuries at our disposal have failed to reduce the level of stress and anxiety in our lives. We are the most stressed generation ever, despite having no imminent threat to life, as many previous generations did.

Statistics reveal that 73% of all working adults experience varying degrees of stress in their daily lives (Walter et al., 2021).

One of the biggest reasons for job change in the modern world is not the temptation of a better salary or benefits package, but stress. Even kids are suffering from a great deal of stress these days.

Stress, anxiety, and worry have become a common part of the modern lifestyle. Our stress levels remain unusually high even in situations when there should be no stress at all. We have become naturally unhappy and need specific reasons to be happy. This is the opposite of what should be the norm. It is a very sad state of affairs, and it leads to greater irritability, which creates a vicious cycle: the more irritable you get, the more hostile and unreceptive an environment you'll create for yourself, leading to even more stress.

If you find yourself becoming irritable on a regular basis, the best solution is to move away from the problem for a while and give yourself time to decompress and relax. There will be times when the tunnel of anxiety seems endless, but remember that everything has an end, and that includes the things that are causing you anxiety. Consistent overthinking and stress can lead to feelings of guilt and worthlessness, so you need to constantly remind yourself that the situation isn't permanent and doesn't define you. Positive affirmations and spending time on creative pursuits are two good ways to overcome these negative feelings.

Impact on Sleep

Are you plagued by worries that seem to bombard your brain as soon as your head hits the pillow? Do you lie awake for hours at night, overthinking every aspect of your life? You're certainly not alone. Lack of sleep due to overthinking is a common phenomenon. While it's true that everyone has valid problems or stressors, the important thing is how you deal with them. Life is just too short to worry about the small things!

The reason you seem to suddenly have hundreds of negative or stressful thoughts when you try to go to bed is because your brain is less distracted at night. This is the time that you can relax, and your mind is calmer. During the day, because we tend to be very busy, our brains just brush off the deeper or more anxious thoughts we may have.

However, this isn't something you want to ignore until the lack of sleep grows out of control. Sleep is crucial for all human beings to live healthy lives. It's important for adults to get approximately eight hours of restful sleep every night. If we fail to get sufficient sleep, we'll become even more stressed and anxious. A bad sleep cycle can affect everything else we do, and if one bad cycle leads to another and another, you may end up dealing with insomnia—which is linked to depression.

Sleeplessness and insomnia take a heavy toll on a person's mind. For instance, one study of over 2,000 participants reported that tiredness and constant fatigue were associated with high stress levels (Rolle et al., 2019). Similarly, another study found that people who had high levels of stress related to their work tended to experience restlessness before bed and increased sleepiness throughout the day (Van Someren, 2021). Yet another study, consisting of over 2,000 participants, found that people who experienced higher numbers of stressful events were at an increased risk of insomnia (Hackett et al., 2020). Thus, you can see how important it is to manage both your stress and your sleep to protect your health.

Impact on Work

When Jessie saw the time, she panicked. She'd been working on this project for days, sitting in front of her computer and just staring at the blank document for what felt like forever. Now there were only a few hours to go before she had to hand in the final project, and she was an anxious mess. The document was still nearly completely empty, and some very important clients were waiting for her work on the other side of her screen.

But Jessie was a perfectionist—or so she told herself. Every little detail of the project had to be perfect, so every time she'd been about to add something, she found herself wondering if it was the right choice. She was petrified of messing everything up. If she messed up the project, she would in turn mess up her relationship with the client, which could end in losing that client. And if she lost the client, they might speak badly about her to others, which could lead to her losing more clients, which would in turn ruin her career. Without a career, she wouldn't be able to afford her apartment; she'd end up living on the streets, maybe even worse. So, every time Jessie looked at the project, she spent way too much time examining every choice from every possible angle, trying to figure out every single thing that could go wrong and prevent it from happening.

Because of this, Jessie ended up working till the last minute, making rushed choices just to finish in time. All the things she'd been mulling over had to be decided on a whim, and when the project was finally handed in, she found herself praying that she'd made the right choices, that she wouldn't lose her client or her job.

Because she overthought every step of the project, Jessie wasted a lot of time simply thinking instead of doing, which made the whole project take longer than it should have to complete. If she had been more assertive and trusted herself more, the project would've taken considerably less time, which means she could have taken more projects. This mindset not only wastes time, it also creates high levels of anxiety.

A state of anxiety may be short-lived and decrease after a stressful event ends, or it may manifest as part of an individual's temperament. If you're not usually nervous, but a specific event—for example, the birth of your first child— causes you to suddenly experience anxiety, which then fades after the event is over, you're anxious. On the other hand, if you tend to feel anxious all the time, it could be one of your personality traits, or you may be experiencing an anxiety disorder.

Being constantly tired can be a symptom of overthinking as well. Your body needs you to pay attention to the signals it's sending rather than continue to go about your day and ignore its important messages. While fatigue can be caused by overworking, overthinking can also wear you out. Pushing your brain to the limit eventually leads to burnout.

Unfortunately, job security is not a luxury we can all afford. It's natural to worry about being out of a job, especially when it could happen with no warning. Everyone has had anxious thoughts about how they would afford bills and other financial responsibilities without a steady paycheck. Add external forces such as the competitive job market to the pressure of work, and the worries seem endless. However, you must not let this genuine cause for concern overwhelm you and affect your productivity—or your peace of mind—at work.

Impact on Energy Levels

The baby was crying, the toddler had scattered his Legos all across the floor, and a burning smell was coming from the kitchen. Linda ran to the oven and pulled out the nearly-scorched dinner, almost burning herself in the process and struggling not to curse out loud. It wasn't too bad; a little extra sauce and she could make do.

It had been such a long day, and the truth was, Linda was exhausted. She wanted to curl up in bed and sleep, but there was still so much to do. So many things on her never-ending list.

It had been a while since Linda stopped working to dedicate herself full-time to her family—not out of necessity, but because she wanted to. It was a pleasure for her at the start, and her husband was able to provide for the family, which was great. All Linda had wanted was to spend more quality time with their kids, to be there for them. But nowadays, she couldn't stop worrying. There were always so many things on her mental to-do list: laundry, groceries, caring for the kids, organizing their toys, cleaning the house, and on and on. The problem was that Linda could never choose what to do first. Instead, she kept wavering back and forth about what would be best for her kids, for her husband, for her overall agenda.

At the end of each day, Linda would find she'd only done half the things she needed to do, but still, she was so tired. Her mind felt cluttered, she had a headache from all the thinking, and all she wanted to do was sleep. So, when her toddler came up to her after dinner and asked her to read him a story before bed, Linda said, "Tomorrow, baby. Mommy's too tired today. Just go to sleep."

The problem in this case is that instead of being proactive, organizing her tasks, and then tackling them one by one, Linda spent too much time thinking about what to do first. This exhausted her mentally, and she ended up failing to achieve the one thing that she wanted when she made the choice to stay at home full-time: spending more time with her kids.

Overthinking can become a part of your psyche and affect you physically until you address it head-on. It will manifest itself as muscle and joint pain without any medical cause. Although overthinking starts in your head, it eventually affects everything in your body, causing exhaustion, fatigue, aches and pains. To avoid this, one strategy is to exercise regularly and stretch before going to sleep. This will not only help you achieve a healthy body, but also help to quiet your mind.

Overthinking starts off in the brain, but it impacts us physically and emotionally as well, leaving us feeling sluggish and exhausted (Hill, 2019). The mind and body are closely related—so much so that a decline in one will negatively affect the other. When a person is under high levels of prolonged stress, they can experience decreased energy levels and chronic fatigue. Similarly, if your body is in pain, it affects your emotions. You will continue to experience stress and pain unless the main culprit is addressed.

Key Takeaways

- Overthinkers want to be perfectionists in everything they do. They can't face failure and make efforts to avoid it at all costs. The fear of failure paralyzes the overthinker so much that they would rather do nothing at all to ensure they don't fail.

- Falling asleep is a challenge for all overthinkers. Overthinking takes away your ability to slow your racing thoughts. The mind becomes too stimulated for sleep. Worries and regrets plague your mind, and you can't escape from your mental hell. All of this comes together to create the perfect recipe for insomnia.

- If you have headaches often, you may be thinking too much. Headaches tell our bodies that we need a break. This applies to our brains as well. Pay attention to your thoughts and see if you think the same things repeatedly. Worriers tend to have negative looping thought systems, so to counter this, try to catch those negative thoughts and gradually replace them with positive ones.

- Being constantly tired is a signal from your body that there's a problem you need to solve. While fatigue can be caused by overworking, overthinking can also wear you out and cause burnout.

Time to Take Action

Analyze your sleep habits and pay attention to how long it takes you to fall asleep or how many times you wake up in the middle of the night. Now that you're aware of this, ask yourself what thoughts you're having during these times, and try to replace those thoughts with something else while falling asleep. Overthinking can consume your mind if you let it, so if you try to focus on something else while you're drifting off, it will be easier for your mind to quiet down and fall asleep.

The next time you have a headache, instead of ignoring it or taking an aspirin, as most people do, take the time to slow down and think about what could be causing it. Are you overthinking and stressing yourself out? Take a break and try to relax.

If you're constantly tired, even after getting the proper amount of sleep, it's possible that overthinking is behind this problem. Even if you get plenty of sleep, you'll completely drain yourself of energy if you're always stressing about something. This type of overthinking often stems from worrying about the present or the future. Next time you find this happening, try to calm yourself in the moment and remind yourself that worrying won't actually solve your problems.

When I was a teenager, upon the request of my mother, I read Psalm 6 almost every night. It's one of my favorite Psalms to this day. In this Psalm, we see that David was experiencing some sleepless nights. He writes:

> *"I am weary with my groaning;*
> *All night I make my bed swim;*
> *I drench my couch with my tears."*
>
> **– Psalm 6:6 (NKJV)**

When you read the full Psalm, you'll find there is a change of tone at the end. David did not stay long in this situation of sleeplessness and overthinking. Instead, he talked to his God, and he received the firm assurance that God would take control of his life. He adds:

> *"Depart from me, all you workers of iniquity;*
> *For the Lord has heard the voice of my weeping.*
> *The Lord has heard my supplication;*
> *The Lord will receive my prayer."*
>
> **– Psalm 6:8, 9 (NKJV)**

There may be a situation in your life at this very moment that's keeping you awake at night. As you read this book, I hope you can see that there is hope for you. Just as David cried out to God, you, too, can cry out to Him! He will hear your voice and receive your prayer, and eventually you will be able to say, like David:

*"This poor man cried out, and the Lord heard him,
And saved him out of all his troubles."*

– Psalm 34:6 (NKJV)

Now we've started to piece together the big picture of overthinking, its impact on the body and mind, and the need to stop it. Finally, we will examine its social effects.

PART III

Social Effects

"Yea, though I walk through the valley of the shadow of death, I will fear no evil; For You are with me"

– **Psalm 23:4 (NKJV)**

Do you ever feel that you think too much about what people say to you or think about you? Do you worry about whether they're laughing at your jokes… or laughing at you? Overthinking can affect not just you, but also the people around you. Here's an example of the social consequences of overthinking:

Matt was a workaholic. He spent more time at the office than any of his colleagues. Often, he would arrive twenty minutes early and leave one hour later than everyone else. He took on more responsibilities than he ever should, and he chose to take on many tasks unnecessarily. Why? Well, Matt was a worrier. He worried constantly about his financial future, about being able to provide for his family. It took over his thoughts and drove him to work overtime—literally—to try to avoid the financial hardship he feared so much.

Even after he became financially very comfortable thanks to all the hard work, he continued to work overtime—at the expense of his family. Matt hardly ever went home to be with them. To deal with the stress of work, he would go out every night and get drunk with his buddies, stay out until 4 a.m., and then stumble back home in the middle of the night. His behavior, driven by fear and overthinking, led to a nightmare for him. His wife left him and got a divorce, and she took the children from him.

Matt was left alone. He sold the beautiful house he'd bought for his family and got a one-bedroom apartment. Matt learned the hard way that he could not let his anxiety take over, causing him to neglect his relationships. He eventually became less fear-driven and more focused on developing a good rapport with people. Instead of constantly working, he chose to do the things he needed to do and then give himself time for recreation and relaxation. Instead of getting drunk every night, he chose to spend some time in silence, relaxing and cultivating a peaceful mind, which made a big difference in his overall lifestyle. He began to worry less about money and to focus on what was important: living a meaningful life.

Relationships are difficult for everyone. When you add worrying and overthinking to the mix, the results can be disastrous. Relationships can be ruined if one person worries or overthinks excessively. The mind of the anxious person plays tricks on them. They can't help but overanalyze every word their partner says, every look, every eye roll, every gesture. They pick up on little things that might not mean anything, think about them continuously, and create problems in their mind. They might even consistently ignore their own needs to please their partner because they're worried about what might happen if they don't.

If this sounds like you, understand that it isn't your fault. It's just how your brain has been programmed—and you have the power to reprogram it.

Impact on Time

To put it bluntly, overthinking is a waste of time. It can cause you to miss out on so many things in life. Are you missing out on new relationships because you overanalyze every new person you meet? Does worry impact your work and cause you to underachieve? Do you spend hours stressing about past or future events when you could be putting that time to more productive use?

The world is so full of possibilities, and while it's true that some of those possibilities are negative, there are many positive opportunities out there. Don't spend your precious time worrying about the worst possible outcomes.

Here is the problem with this type of thinking: most of us will have negative experiences in life (issues with maintaining a healthy weight, failing an exam, messing up at work, getting rejected by someone); however, we'll also have positive experiences (being successful in a loving relationship, achieving something great at work, enjoying good times with friends). It is only through experiencing and learning from both positive *and* negative events that we can grow as people and evolve into better versions of ourselves. Trying to avoid negative experiences altogether is just a waste of time and effort.

If you can't live in the moment and appreciate life as it comes because you're overthinking so much, you'll lose track of the world and live entirely in your mind. Being constantly stuck in your own head distances you from others. Make an effort to open up your mind and heart to those around you and avoid getting stuck in cycles of negative thinking. Focus on thinking positively and ignore the negative thoughts that bring you down.

For those who can live in the moment rather than in their thoughts, the world offers many opportunities for amazing personal interactions and experiences, as well as connections with others who can assist in quieting that negative inner voice. True friendships allow us to redirect our attention away from ourselves and our negative thoughts so that we can concentrate on the needs of others.

Learn to listen to other people—those who can help and support you. Form bonds with them, and learn more about them. Wasting time with chronic overthinking is a problem that you can solve by creating a strong community around you and learning from and supporting each other.

Impact on Joy

Overthinking is a joy-killer. It causes the unconscious regions of your brain to misinterpret what is reality versus what are just thoughts. As a result, when you're stressed by something, your body perceives the threat as real. Experts note that while overthinking may appear to be relaxing at first (anxiety levels tend to drop initially because we believe we are well-prepared for the threat), it turns out that the more we overthink, the higher our anxiety levels get, creating a vicious cycle. And as our stress levels drop, our happiness and joy increase.

Impact on Self-Esteem

People who battle with almost every little decision are more likely to suffer from low self-esteem. This feeling of low self-worth can impact your life in many ways, and is also a sign of generalized anxiety disorder (GAD), which can have long-term consequences.

Our self-esteem is shaped by how we perceive other people's reactions to us. As a result, people who experience a lot of acceptance from others have higher self-esteem, whereas those who experience a lot of rejection have lower self-esteem.

Nevertheless, you are still the only person with the power to change your self-esteem—even if it's very low.

To change your self-esteem, try analyzing the levels of acceptance and rejection you experience. While we often focus on negative situations, such as people being rude or someone avoiding us, we tend to overlook all the people who care for us and with whom we have positive interactions. Take a close look at the number of people in your life who care for you. Most folks will find there are significantly more people who accept them than reject them, which should translate into better feelings and higher self-esteem (Suhaimi, 2020).

If you have anxiety, your stress and worrying can be exhausting. Seeking therapy and help from God can help manage your symptoms and improve your interpersonal relationships. Please remember that if you lack belief in yourself because of what has happened to you in the past, have a little trust in the people around you! Let them plant you in front of the mirror and tell you how beautiful you are, inside and out.

Key Takeaways

- Overthinking disarms our ability to perform. When you're an overthinker, you'll often find yourself wasting time just focusing on your negative thoughts. When you give that negativity the chance to stay in your mind for some time, it affects your creativity and productivity because, instead of doing important or meaningful things, you're paralyzed by anxiety and lose valuable time.

- One of the trademarks of being an overthinker is having a "negativity bias," which means you fixate on insults and criticisms and ignore positive interactions with others. This tendency teaches our brain to register and dwell on negative stimuli only. Overthinkers find it hard to think of ways to move forward and take better action, and their negativity bias kills their joy.

- Overthinkers are less likely to take chances and more likely to live life in the "should" zone instead of the "could" zone, which affects their long-term goals and career.

Time to Take Action

Don't overthink. Of course, that's easier said than done, but it's important to remember that not every problem has to be solved, and sometimes a problem actually can't be solved by you. It may be something you just need to let take its course. In any case, overthinking it won't help and will only make your anxiety worse.

If you find yourself worrying too much and obsessing over the worst-case scenario, try to find ways to stop your mind from honing in on the fear and instead think of constructive solutions.

Be positive. When you focus on the positive aspects of a situation, you can turn off your negative thoughts and solve problems with more clarity and optimism.

Forgive yourself for being an overthinker. Everyone makes mistakes, especially in this complex world, and the important thing is that you move forward instead of getting stuck in the past.

In the midst of your chaotic world, God wants to give you joy. It seems like a paradox, right? But believe me, it's possible through the Holy Spirit. The Thessalonians were experiencing bad days, but Paul wrote to them and reassured them:

> *"You became followers of us and of the Lord,*
> *having received the word in much affliction, with joy of the Holy Spirit."*
>
> **– 1 Thessalonians 1:6 (NKJV)**

God has already promised this power to you. The only thing you have to do is to ask and reclaim this promise with faith in the name of Jesus. It's time to come out of this sea of overthinking, where you are continually floundering.

For more tips and strategies on overthinking and codependency check out my other books on Amazon. **Click this link**

https://www.amazon.com/Robert-JCharles/e/B092DLKRYH?geniuslink=true

PART IV

Moving Forward

"Do not sorrow, for the joy of the Lord is your strength."

– Nehemiah 8:10 (NKJV)

Jake was having a mid-life crisis. Or so he thought. His job paid well, yet he was constantly worrying about his finances. He approached the end of each month with increasing trepidation. His bills, although they were just a fraction of his salary, had him stressed most of the time. It wasn't that he couldn't afford to pay them; he just couldn't stop thinking about them.

Things didn't get better after the company Jake worked for hired a new guy. On the surface, it was a great thing; the new employee was friendly, easygoing, and made Jake's workload easier. But Jake had become increasingly fearful about his job security. He believed the new guy was his replacement and that he would soon be forced to leave the company.

Although his managers had never given any indication that they doubted Jake's competence, Jake had become increasingly critical of himself and full of self-doubt. There was no evidence to support his unfounded fear of getting the sack, yet he became quiet and withdrawn whenever he was at the office. Whenever Jake's boss invited him into his office, he was convinced he was about to be fired. Even if the meeting went well, without any issues, he continued to believe he would get the bad news someday soon.

Jake lived under this dark cloud daily, expecting the worst but trying to hide his feelings. Spurred on by persistent feelings of inadequacy, Jake began to volunteer for more tasks at the office and work extra hours. He was convinced that if he put in more effort, upper management would be pleased and his job would no longer be threatened by the newcomer. Over time, Jake became a yes-man, willing to do anything just to please his superiors and protect his job.

Soon, Jake couldn't find time to rest. From the moment he opened his eyes to the moment he hit the sack, he was buried in paperwork that hardly made any sense to him. Gradually, he began to fall behind schedule, miss deadlines, and turn up late for the appointments he managed to remember. All of these issues only served to compound his worries and drive him closer to the edge.

As if things couldn't get any worse for Jake, he received an invite to the wedding of one of his college friends. While he was happy for the lucky couple, he couldn't help but believe he had failed in life. He began to think of his past two relationships and wondered if he had put in enough effort. In time, he began to notice flaws in his current relationship with Sandra. He was convinced that he wasn't good enough for her, and she would be dumping him in good time.

Money problems, work problems, and relationship issues. Jake seemed to have it worse than everyone else around him. He wondered if he should be putting in more effort. He even doubted whether he was putting in any effort at all.

Soon, Jake could no longer cope with all the stress he had to deal with. He became highly suspicious of his colleagues at the office and was convinced that they were all in some kind of conspiracy to make his life miserable. He would sit at home at the end of each day wondering what subtle messages they were trying to send him when they made positive remarks about his looks or complimented his work. At night, he tossed and turned in bed, unable to sleep while he worried about what they might be thinking about him.

He became easily triggered and could spend several hours lost in his thoughts. Eventually, he needed pills to help him relax and calm his racing heart. He carried them with him wherever he went. Not feeling his bottle of pills in his pocket could send Jake into violent panic attacks that left him incoherent for some time.

Does Jake's sad story remind you of someone? You see, just like Jake, you might find yourself trapped in the deadly cycle of overthinking. And though you're surrounded by lots of evidence to contradict your thinking, you refuse to see things any other way.

The only threat to Jake's job existed solely in his mind. The only sack letter he was going to get was the one he wrote to himself. The only person conspiring against him was himself. With his overthinking, Jake had set off a toxic spiral that would end up destroying him.

If you're anything like Jake, you overthink so much that you can no longer sleep at night, and even when you manage to snatch a few hours here and there, you wake up feeling restless and more exhausted. Your attitude towards life and people around you is shaped by the negative results of your overthinking, and you can no longer hold a positive perspective on your life circumstances. You may have also dismissed the obvious symptoms of the effect of overthinking on your health. Chances are that you have denied yourself the opportunity to enjoy the high-quality and wholesome relationships in your life by being increasingly suspicious of every person around you and holding on to imagined grudges.

Take a moment to imagine sliding down a spiral slide without any stops. You are simply going around in a circle without any end in sight. That's the same way it feels when you allow overthinking to take over your life. Unlike Jake, you may have just one issue that causes you to overthink. However, regardless of the cause, you must not let overthinking become a part of your life.

In the previous chapters of this book, you have discovered the dangers of overthinking. In this chapter, you will discover proven strategies that you can use to put an end to overthinking. You need to face it. Overthinking will never just stop or go away on its own. You need to take the bull by the horns and address it head-on if you hope to make any progress.

Are you wondering whether it is possible for you to ever break free of overthinking? The answer is yes, it is. Nobody is born an overthinker. This toxic behavior is something that you may have subconsciously learned. It might also be a form of self-defense that you adopted early in life to cope with stress or abuse. Therefore, you can unlearn this behavior and get rid of it completely by taking strategic steps.

In this chapter, you will also find techniques you can use to develop and maintain a healthy mindset, which will fully equip you to set off on the path towards the life you desire.

Effective Strategies to Stop Overthinking

Stopping your tendency to overthink is a crucial step in living the best life you could ever imagine. However, you cannot just snap your fingers and expect that to put an end to this toxic habit. If you truly want to free yourself of this menace and take control of your thoughts and emotions, you need to commit to applying these proven strategies consistently.

1. Get New Hobbies

Learning a new hobby is a great way to invest your mental energy into something positive and focus your mind on more productive ventures. Did you know that when you learn a new skill, you stimulate the neurons in your brain and form fresh neural pathways? By building these new pathways, you keep your mind sharper and more focused. You also reduce your chances of developing dementia.

You can choose to learn a new language, immerse yourself in history, or learn a new musical instrument. You could also choose to learn a new skill. As long as it is something entirely new to you, it will help you get your mind off unproductive thoughts.

When choosing a new hobby, pick an activity that is unrelated to your career or line of work. However, the hobby should be something you are passionate about so you won't get bored. Also, try to pick something that isn't common among members of your close circle of friends and family. This reduces the likelihood that you'll engage in unhealthy competition later on.

2. Volunteer

Many researchers agree that idle minds provide the most fertile ground for overthinking. The Bible says an idle mind is the devil's workshop. However, by volunteering your skills and resources for good causes, you can eliminate the chances of overthinking. Volunteering helps you get more time off your hands and leaves you with little or no time to be overwhelmed by persistent negative thoughts. It also brings you in contact with more people and broadens your perspective.

You can find lots of charity organizations and NGOs online that would greatly profit from your skillset. However, you could also look around you and find several needs you could meet within your community. Remember, we think less about ourselves when we put more of ourselves into the service of others.

3. Seek Therapy

Most times, the only way to put an end to persistent overthinking is by speaking up. Keeping your worries and negative emotions locked in will only leave you feeling worse with every passing minute. Instead, you should open up and receive professional advice about dealing with the issues that are bothering you.

There is sufficient proof to show that merely talking about the problems you have is therapeutic. Besides, expressing your worries by way of speech will also help you put your thoughts into a better perspective. This way, solving them becomes a whole lot easier.

4. Forgive and Forget

Sometimes, your overthinking is a product of repressed guilt and emotions that you are trying so hard to hold on to. Perhaps you have a long-held resentment against your parents for something they did while you were growing up, or you're upset with your spouse for missing an important anniversary. Maybe you even get angry at yourself for some cringeworthy moment you can't forget.

Well, you could choose to hold on to these grudges and continue to overthink the events surrounding them. Or, you can let go of them instead for the sake of your mental well-being. Holding on to offenses will only leave you feeling more resentment whenever you think of them. If you are not careful, you might even resort to self-harm.

5. Write Down Your Thoughts

Putting your thoughts into writing is also a productive exercise that will help you overcome overthinking. It is often difficult—even impossible—to keep track of your thoughts when you are overthinking. Hence, you may find yourself thinking in endless circles without making any real progress.

However, when you put your thoughts in writing, you give them a sense of order and structure. Writing down your thoughts also helps you evaluate them more quickly. This way, you can strike out any irrelevant or unproductive thoughts and reach effective decisions in good time.

6. Take Action

Most of the time, we overthink things because we are too timid to act on decisions we have already made. In the end, we are left to deal with unnecessary stress that we could have avoided by simply getting the job done. Inaction leads to overthinking.

Instead of overthinking, have that discussion. Call that person. Send that invitation. Just do it. Allowing your mind to play out imaginary events will never influence their outcome. However, taking the bold step and putting the source of your overthinking behind you will save you lots of valuable energy.

7. Practice Gratitude

Overthinking typically leaves you with negative thoughts and feelings, and first among these feelings of negativity is ingratitude. When you overthink things, you might begin to believe that others have it better than you, or that your opportunities are inadequate.

You might also take offense at inanimate objects and blame them for perceived misfortunes rather than being grateful for them. You could blame the sun for ruining your day or the wind for not blowing to cool you down in the heat.

To overcome overthinking, you must replace such feelings with gratitude instead. Mentally appreciate the people around you who do remarkable things rather than feel left out. Be grateful for nature's gifts instead of holding grudges against them. Once you develop a grateful mindset, you limit the opportunity for your thoughts to spiral into an endless blame game.

8. Identify Your Triggers

You can also overcome overthinking by identifying the events that might trigger your thoughts. For many people, being alone is all they need to descend into the vicious pit of overthinking. For others, however, their triggers might be idleness, stress, insomnia, sickness, or a combination of several other factors.

Identify your triggers and avoid them completely. Unfortunately, you might find some of these triggers impossible to avoid. If you can't avoid any of the triggers you identify, you could prepare yourself mentally to overcome them whenever you encounter them.

9. Give Yourself Credit

Most overthinkers are the topic of their own overthinking, and usually not in a good way. Overthinkers often subject themselves to harsh and unfair criticism. They also continually question their worth and abilities.

Dwelling on self-deprecating thoughts will lower your self-esteem and affect your relationships with others. However, you can put an end to that vicious cycle by recognizing your strengths and dwelling on them instead. You are awesome, not messed up. You can learn; you're not "good for nothing."

Once you begin to give yourself some credit, you will have an easier time letting go of any unwholesome beliefs that you might have about yourself.

10. Let Go of the Past

You need to draw the curtains on your past. No amount of overthinking will ever change what has happened. Take any lessons that you find with good faith, and move on with your life.

Stop worrying about what might have happened if you had done or said something different. Quit beating yourself up over some mistake you made so many years ago. Stop replaying that nasty confrontation you got into at the last family gathering. Leave the past exactly where it is—behind you.

11. Think Positively

Overthinking thrives amid negativity. Once your mind gets hold of a single negative thought and you choose to dwell on it, you'll likely find it impossible to stop that single thought from turning into more negative and increasingly graphic offshoots. You can put an end to this menace by thinking positive thoughts instead.

For example, if you are dreading a performance review meeting with your boss at work, begin to think of the meeting as the next step to securing a promotion or higher pay. Stop thinking about getting fired or being saddled with more responsibility. While thinking positively may not determine the outcome of anything, it equips you with a healthier mindset and saves you a lot of stress.

12. Seek Closure

A lot of your overthinking might be due to incorrect assumptions you have about certain events or even other people. You may have misinterpreted a gesture, mistook something someone said, or possibly overreacted to a harmless overture. Hence, you might find yourself continually overthinking the situation and imagining nonexistent things.

To get past the dark clouds of doubt such situations leave you with, you should seek closure immediately. Overthinking will only leave you with the wrong answers. Instead, have that discussion. Raise that question. Seek clarity. This way, you tie up loose ends and save yourself from needless mental torture.

13. Take Reality Checks

What are the chances of being turned away from your favorite restaurant because you complimented the chef? Or the chances of meeting a lion in the restroom when you take a bathroom break?

When you are caught in the vicious cycle of overthinking, it becomes increasingly difficult for you to draw a line between fiction and reality. Often, this leads to developing unrealistic expectations or even reaching impossible conclusions. Hence, you must take regular reality checks.

Getting a reality check involves breaking down your persistent thoughts into smaller ones that you can evaluate separately. When you have done this, cross out the impossibilities that constantly plague you. You could also put down your thoughts on a sheet of paper and eliminate the unrealistic ones as you assess the list.

14. Exercise

Staying idle is a very common trigger for overthinking. One way you could make the most of your idle time is by exercising. You could go for a short walk or jog around the neighborhood. If the conditions do not allow for outdoor exercise, pick any indoor exercise routine you are cool with.

Remember, the goal is to occupy your mind with healthier alternatives, so no need to wear yourself out. You could also engage in other physical activities such as cleaning your home or doing chores.

Besides reducing overthinking, constant exercise also puts you in a better position to improve your general well-being.

15. Recognize Your Limits

There are some things that you might never be able to control, no matter how long or hard you overthink them. It's okay to acknowledge this fact, and it takes nothing away from your self-worth. Instead, it puts you in a better position to leverage your strengths.

Instead of overthinking the negative effects of cold weather, get warm. Instead of overthinking the possibility of a sunburn, find suitable shade. When you fail to recognize your limits, you expend your energy on unproductive ventures. In the end, you are left with nothing to show for your efforts.

16. Practice Self-Acceptance

A lot of your overthinking may be triggered by feelings of inadequacy or low self-esteem. You might think nobody likes you, or everyone at work is trying to avoid you, or nobody would like to hear your opinion about anything at all. All of these signs are indications that you are not at peace with yourself.

You may do things wrong from time to time, but that doesn't mean that you are a mistake. Refuse to believe such demeaning things about yourself.

Consciously practice self-acceptance by identifying your strengths, but also, admit any weaknesses and commit to working on them. The next step is to practice self-affirmation to help you reject any bad perceptions you might hold about your person and only allow wholesome opinions.

17. Live in the Moment

Overthinking denies you the opportunity to enjoy the present. It forces you to constantly rehash past events or draw unrealistic pictures about the future. Choose to live in the moment instead. Focus on the now. You cannot change the past nor bring the future any faster than it should come. But by taking advantage of the present, you can set your life on the path you desire.

18. Avoid Comparisons

It is difficult to overcome overthinking when you're continually comparing yourself to other people. You're likely creating unrealistic yardsticks of comparison based on your perception of these people and beating yourself up when you fail to measure up to these warped standards. By continually comparing yourself to others, you'll lose sight of your strengths and resort to constant self-criticism.

Put an end to needless comparisons. If there is anyone you should be competing with, that person is you. You should continually strive for self-improvement rather than engaging in unhealthy competition with others. Set SMART goals for yourself that allow you to measure your progress yourself. This way, you can make real progress.

19. Breathe, Slowly and Deeply

Overthinking creates a lot of anxiety, which could lead to the development of several symptoms including heart palpitations. This condition triggers the release of hormones that will only leave you feeling worse with each passing second.

You can avoid this problem by taking slow, deep breaths that return your body to a state of calm. Start with 10 deep breaths. Count them as you go. You can slow down the rate and take deeper breaths as you progress. Remember, the goal is to focus on your immediate well-being and to stop your thoughts from racing.

20. Immerse Yourself in Nature

It is easy to stop paying attention to nature as you deal with hectic schedules and try to meet deadlines. Making an effort to appreciate nature's gifts will fill your mind with healthier mental fodder for your thoughts. Besides shifting your focus from unhealthy thoughts, immersing yourself in nature will also fill you with gratitude.

Spend time looking out your windows and admiring the blooming flowers, the trees, and the birds. Take a walk in the park, smell the roses, and enjoy the feel of the wind on your skin. Nature is free, and so are its gifts. They are yours for the taking. Enjoy them.

How to Develop and Maintain a Healthy Mindset

One of the most effective ways to protect yourself from the harmful consequences of overthinking is to develop a healthy mindset. With such a mindset, you'll be able to approach situations from a more positive perspective and reduce the occurrence of negative thoughts.

It is easy to identify the components of a healthy mindset; they include a "can-do" attitude, empathy, and respect for the needs and feelings of others. With a healthy mindset, it will be easier for you to attract positive feelings and energy. It will also equip you with the perspective you need to navigate any negative situations you might encounter.

A healthy mindset might not fix your life instantly, but it can make all the difference between an unhappy life and a joyful one. You can begin the process of freeing yourself of the heavy burdens of an unhealthy mindset by applying the following strategies.

1. Shut Out the Noise

Trying to focus on too many things at once will leave you stressed out. Therefore, you must focus only on what matters. Find your priorities and channel your energy towards them.

Also, if you're constantly dealing with lots of opinions and unsolicited advice, it becomes difficult to reach quick and effective conclusions. You don't need a thousand opinions to reach a decision. Learn to filter out negative opinions about yourself and what you do, and only take what is useful.

2. Surround Yourself with Quality People

Your mindset is a reflection of the people you associate with. If you are in constant company with naysayers or overthinkers, it will be difficult for you to maintain a healthy mindset. They will always find problems where there are none and never find anything positive about any situation. Remember, misery loves company.

However, if you begin to interact with positive people who try to make the best of every situation, you will notice significant improvements in your mindset.

3. Create a Routine

Research shows that introducing a sense of order to your daily activities significantly reduces the chances of developing anxiety and other stress-related diseases. Besides saving time and helping you channel your resources more effectively, working with a routine puts you in a state of preparedness and increases your confidence.

While you may not be able to follow a strict routine for your entire day, you can adopt a routine that guides your waking hours, allowing you to take control of your morning and giving a sense of direction to the rest of your day.

4. Get Adequate Sleep

You are not doing yourself any favors by denying your brain enough sleep. Studies have shown that people need about eight hours of sleep to function properly. Without adequate sleep, you may find yourself on edge most of the time and unable to focus. You might also seek solace in caffeine and energy drinks, but that will only make things worse. Get a sleeping schedule that works for you, and give up any distractions that prevent you from following it. Ask yourself if the reason you're staying up late is worth the sleep deprivation.

5. Stop Procrastinating

Start taking immediate action—quit procrastinating. Postponing things you should do now till later will not make them any easier. Also, when you procrastinate, you are more likely to develop stress and anxiety as deadlines approach.

You may be tempted to give lots of excuses for your procrastination, such as indecision, lack of motivation, or the desire for perfection. But know that making procrastination a habit will weaken your resolve to act on anything, and this will negatively affect your self-esteem.

6. Set Boundaries

The key to maintaining a healthy mindset is to take charge of the influences you allow around you. Therefore, you need to set clear personal boundaries. Without boundaries, you'll have to put up with lots of unacceptable behavior from the people around you. When you set clear boundaries, you limit such occurrences and reduce the amount of negative influence you are forced to deal with.

7. Eat Healthily

Your body and mind work in sync to influence your living standards. Therefore, you can develop a healthy mindset by giving your body the right nourishment.

Besides cutting down on your intake of junk food and high-sugar-content drinks, you should also eat more fruits and vegetables. These natural foods contain essential nutrients that could reduce anxiety-related symptoms and leave you feeling better all around.

Also, hydrate your body regularly to dilute the concentration of any toxins your brain produces while under stress.

8. Quit Bad Habits

It is impossible to have a healthy mindset while holding on to bad habits. You can't find a compromise that allows positive and negative energy to exist in the same space. It simply cannot work.

Besides the obvious destructive habits like drug abuse and self-harm, there are others that you need to quit right away. For example, watching movies late into the night or binge eating will add no value to your life. Instead, they will leave you drained in the long run. To some people, these habits may seem like nothing to worry about, but if you wish to maintain a healthy mindset, you must do away with these unproductive habits right away.

9. Practice Effective Communication

Thoughts translate into words. Hence, it is often difficult to express your opinions correctly when your thoughts are largely negative or out of control. Fortunately, you can reshape your mindset by taking control of your words.

You can begin by purging your vocabulary of all forms of unwholesome language and negativity. Next, adopt an approach that matches the character you want to identify with. For example, get rid of the yelling, fist-pounding, and uncontrolled tirades. Make room for others to contribute to the conversation while you listen. Remember, communication goes both ways.

10. Take Breaks

Continuous worry and overthinking could cause long-term and permanent damage to your mental health. However, you can handle stressful situations more efficiently by taking breaks. Find time to rest. Do not allow any project to take an excessive mental toll on you. There's no point in working till you drop dead.

Take time away from work to allow your mind to recuperate and develop fresh ideas—and don't misinterpret the term "breaks" as referring to weekends or summer vacations only. You should be taking regular breaks during your workday as well. Sometimes, a five-minute break at work is all you need to let off excess steam and prevent your thoughts from descending into complete chaos.

11. Never Compromise

You must commit to developing and maintaining a healthy mindset at all times. Leave no room for compromise. You might be struggling with a bad habit or an unwholesome relationship; you might even feel stuck and want to give up on the whole venture. But remember that you are in this for the long-term benefits. Make a list of the improvements you wish to see in your life, and make a mental note of common pitfalls you must avoid. Keep these details in the back of your mind and never let any situation weaken your resolve.

Key Takeaways

- Stopping overthinking is not a straightforward process or a venture you can approach with a one-size-fits-all mindset.
- While you might struggle with implementing some strategies, there are others that will give you the desired results with relative ease.

- However, you must commit to the process and remain consistent throughout.
- Remember, overthinking is a cycle. You need to continually stick to these strategies to avoid being sucked back into that cycle once you escape it.

Time to Take Action

Make a list of the strategies you find most helpful in this chapter. Imagine the difference each of these strategies can make in your life, health, and relationships. Imagine the sort of persona you can create by applying these strategies consistently.

Now, draw up a plan. In this plan, take note of any potential obstacles that could hinder you from applying these strategies consistently. Match these obstacles against the potential benefits you are set to enjoy by applying these strategies. Are they really worth it? Prepare a practical plan for avoiding these obstacles or minimizing their interference with your desired goals. This way, you'll be prepared to deal with these issues as they arise.

Also, be sure to identify your strong points and existing advantages you can leverage to help you make this process easier.

Use a journal to record the results you get from these strategies and track your progress. This will help you to evaluate what works for you and choose which strategies yield the greatest returns.

Never forget:

> *"A merry heart does good, like medicine,*
>
> *but a broken spirit dries the bones."*
>
> **– Proverbs 17:22 (NKJV)**

Conclusion

Overthinking is a silent killer. It begins with a small, insignificant whisper you may find impossible to ignore. As you nurture it, it gradually transforms into a vicious monster that strips you of all sense of control and drags you into a vicious abyss. With time, you'll find it difficult to differentiate between imagination and reality.

When you overthink things, you could eventually warp your perception of real-time events around you. Many people hold on to imaginary offenses over events that never took place. You'll also find lots of people whose health has deteriorated due to the stress and worry that their overthinking causes them. Overthinking won't win you any prizes or do you any favors.

Although many overthinkers recognize the dangers of this toxic habit, they are unable to break free from it. They have become so accustomed to it that they often slip into overthinking unconsciously. For others, overthinking is the only way they can escape harsh realities. Therefore, they readily embrace the short-lived relief that overthinking offers them even though they are aware of the dangers.

However, you can break that cycle right now. You can choose to move forward today.

If you have been troubled by overthinking or are struggling to drop the habit, then you have the key right here in your hands. Take advantage of the 20 techniques you have discovered in this book to escape the vicious web of overthinking. Cultivate a healthy mindset by applying the strategies described in the final chapter of this book.

Sit back for a moment and imagine all the things you can do now that you possess the unlimited power of a healthy mindset.

The choice is yours, dear friend. You can break free of the shackles of overthinking and begin to live a fulfilling and productive life free of mental torture. Right now, you hold the power to take control of your thoughts and go about your endeavors with more focus and clarity.

At this point, you have what it takes to put aside all thoughts of inadequacy or incompetence and be in charge of your dreams. You can keep track of your journey by applying the strategies in this book and keeping detailed records of your progress.

Thank You

I hope you enjoyed this book on the effects of overthinking. My intention in writing this book is to give you a moment to pause and ponder the best decisions you can make to manage your thought processes and avoid overthinking.

If you want to dive deeper into overthinking, and codependency and get more tips and strategies for your personal development, check out my other books on Amazon.

Click [HERE to view my books on Amazon.](#)

References

Ballinger, S. (2022, September 8). *17 effective ways to maintain a healthy mindset.* Sassy Sister Stuff. Retrieved from https://www.sassysisterstuff.com/effective-ways-to-maintain-a-healthy-mindset/

Bergland, C. (2017, June 8). *New research explains why overthinking can hinder creativity.* Psychology Today. Retrieved from https://www.psychologytoday.com/us/blog/the-athletes-way/201706/new-research-explains-why-overthinking-can-hinder-creativity

Cherry, K. (2021, April 8). *5 surprising ways that stress affects your brain.* Verywell Mind. Retrieved from https://www.verywellmind.com/surprising-ways-that-stress-affects-your-brain-2795040

Dahlgren, A., Kecklund, G., & Åkerstedt, T. (2005). Different levels of work-related stress and the effects on sleep, fatigue and cortisol. *Scandinavian Journal of Work, Environment & Health, 31*(4), 277–285. https://doi.org/10.5271/sjweh.883

Facts & Statistics. Anxiety & Depression Association of America. (2021, September 19). Retrieved from https://adaa.org/understanding-anxiety/facts-statistics

Hackett, R. A., Dal, Z., & Steptoe, A. (2020). The relationship between sleep problems and cortisol in people with type 2 diabetes. *Psychoneuroendocrinology*, 117, 104688. https://doi.org/10.1016/j.psyneuen.2020.104688

Hanlon, R. (2022, July 29). *Quiet the anxiety in your head—20 best ways to stop overthinking*. Parade. Retrieved from https://www.parade.com/living/how-to-stop-overthinking/

Hill, K. (2015). Build strength, boost mood, reduce symptoms. *ACSM's Health & Fitness Journal*, *19*(2), 9–13. https://doi.org/10.1249/fit.0000000000000106

Maloney, B. (2020, January 18). *The damaging effects of negativity by Bree Maloney*. Marque Medical. Retrieved from https://marquemedical.com/damaging-effects-of-negativity/

Morin, A. (2017, April 15). *Science says this is what happens when you overthink things*. Inc.com. Retrieved from https://www.inc.com/amy-morin/science-says-this-is-what-happens-when-you-overthink-things.html

Nittle, N. (2021, July 1). *Can social media cause depression?* Verywell Mind. Retrieved from https://www.verywellmind.com/social-media-and-depression-5085354

Raypole, C. (2020, March 17). *Meet anticipatory anxiety, the reason you worry about things that haven't happened yet.* Healthline. Retrieved from https://www.healthline.com/health/anticipatory-anxiety#coping-tips

Rolle, N., Eakman, A., & Graham, J. E. (2019). 0389 When sleep quality improves, do performance and satisfaction in other life roles change. *Sleep, 42*(Supplement_1). https://doi.org/10.1093/sleep/zsz067.388

Suhaimi, N. (2020, March 11). *Overthinking kills happiness and shortens your life.* EMIR Research. Retrieved from https://www.emirresearch.com/overthinking-kills-happiness-and-shortens-your-life/

Van Someren, E. J. (2021). Brain mechanisms of insomnia: New perspectives on causes and consequences. *Physiological Reviews, 101*(3), 995–1046. https://doi.org/10.1152/physrev.00046.2019

Walter, O., Shenaar-Golan, V., & Routray, S. (2021). Cross-cultural comparison of how mind-body practice affects emotional intelligence, cognitive well-being, and mental well-being. *Frontiers in Psychology, 12.* https://doi.org/10.3389/fpsyg.2021.588597

Wolff, C. (2019, March 18). *How negativity actually messes with your brain chemistry.* FabFitFun. Retrieved from https://fabfitfun.com/magazine/negativity-effects-brain-chemistry/

www.ingramcontent.com/pod-product-compliance
Lightning Source LLC
Chambersburg PA
CBHW070742060526
44119CB00071B/125